FUN FACT FILE: FIERCE FISH!

20 FUN FACTS ABOUT STINGRAYS

By Heather Moore Niver

Gareth Stevens
Publishing

Please visit our website, www.garethstevens.com. For a free color catalog of all our high-quality books, call toll free 1-800-542-2595 or fax 1-877-542-2596.

Library of Congress Cataloging-in-Publication Data

Niver, Heather Moore.
20 fun facts about stingrays / Heather Moore Niver.
    p. cm. — (Fun fact file: fierce fish!)
Includes index.
ISBN 978-1-4339-6992-8 (pbk.)
ISBN 978-1-4339-6993-5 (6-pack)
ISBN 978-1-4339-6991-1 (library binding)
1. Stingrays—Juvenile literature. I. Title. II. Title: Twenty fun facts about stingrays.
QL638.8.N58 2012
597.3'5—dc23
                                   2011051420

First Edition

Published in 2013 by
Gareth Stevens Publishing
111 East 14th Street, Suite 349
New York, NY 10003

Copyright © 2013 Gareth Stevens Publishing

Designer: Ben Gardner
Editor: Greg Roza

Photo credits: Cover, pp. 1, 6, 10 Ian Scott/Shutterstock.com; p. 5 tubuceo/Shutterstock.com; p. 7 Wolfgang Poelzer/WaterFrame/Getty Images; p. 8 holbox/Shutterstock.com; pp. 9, 16, 20, 22 © iStockphoto.com/EXTREME-PHOTOGRAPHER; p. 11 Shutterstock.com/Cigdem Sean Cooper; p. 12 Shutterstock.com/Jorge Felix Costa; pp. 13, 24 Shutterstock.com/ Jacek Jasinski; p. 14 emin kuliyev/Shutterstock.com; p. 15 PixAchi/Shutterstock.com; p. 17 Reinhard Dirscherl/WaterFrame/Getty Images; pp. 18–19 ncn18/Shutterstock.com; p. 21 © iStockphoto.com/Island Effects; p. 23 Rich Carey/Shutterstock.com; p. 25 Stephen Coburn/ Shutterstock.com; p. 26 Jeffery L. Rotman/Peter Arnold/Getty Images; p. 27 Colin Keates/ Dorling Kindersley/Getty Images; p. 29 Paul Souders/Photodisc/Getty Images.

Printed in the United States of America

CPSIA compliance information: Batch #CS12GS: For further information contact Gareth Stevens, New York, New York at 1-800-542-2595.

Contents

Words in the glossary appear in **bold** type the first time they are used in the text.

Spiny Stingrays

Stingrays don't look like your average fish. They have a flat, wide body, and most have a long, thin tail. It's that whip-like tail with a **spine** on it that makes stingrays one of the most dangerous fish out there.

Some stingrays are very large. And don't forget strong! They can pull a boat upstream or even sink it. Stingrays may be big and scary, but they're generally gentle. Dive on in and learn more about these flat fish.

Flat Fish

Stingrays are one of the flattest fish in the sea.

Stingrays have such flat bodies that they don't look like most fish. Their bodies look more like disks. Stingrays are so flat they don't even look as if they have a head. Their body shape helps them hide on the sandy sea bottom.

Stingrays are often said to have a kite-shaped body.

Stingrays don't have any bones.

Although sharks and stingrays don't look much alike, they're actually cousins. Neither fish has any bones. Instead, their bodies are supported by cartilage. Cartilage is the stiff, bendable material that's in your ears and the end of your nose.

Hanging Out with Stingrays

FACT 3

Stingrays spend a lot of time just hanging out in the sand.

Not all fish spend their day swimming through the water. Stingrays enjoy chilling out in the sand. Sometimes they bury themselves in the sand to wait for **prey** to swim by. They also bury themselves to hide from **predators**, such as sharks.

Stingrays are usually the same color as the sand, which helps them hide.

Stingrays live in every ocean on the planet.

Stingrays are cold-blooded fish, which means they need warm water to keep their body warm. Most live close to shore in **temperate** or **tropical** waters. They live in every ocean on Earth and in some rivers in South America.

Some stingrays swim by flapping their fins like wings.

Stingrays have **pectoral** fins that run along the whole length of their body. It almost looks as if they have wings rather than fins. In fact, some stingrays flap their fins like wings as they "fly" through the water.

Stingray Sight

A stingray's eyes are perfectly placed for hiding in sand.

The eyes of a stingray are right on top of its head. It might look a little odd, but it helps them see all around. This is handy when they're hiding in the sand. Their mouths are underneath their bodies.

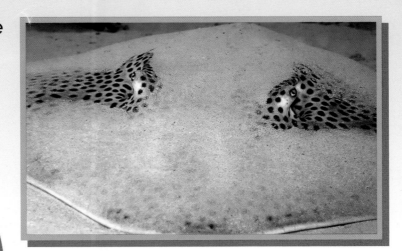

This is a honeycomb whipray.

Stingrays often know when prey swims by without even seeing it.

Although their eyes are placed to see better, scientists don't think stingrays use their sight much to hunt. Instead, they have special **sensors** called the ampullae (am-PU-lee) of Lorenzini. They can sense small electrical charges given off by passing prey.

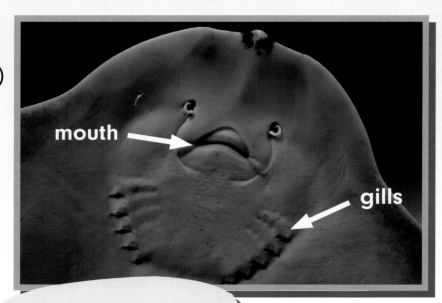

mouth

gills

The ampullae of Lorenzini are located around the stingray's mouth. Sharks have these sensors, too.

spiracles

Special gills help stingrays breathe while they hide in the sand.

Stingrays breathe through **gills** like other fish. The gills are near the mouth on the bottom side of the body. Stingrays also have a special pair of gills called spiracles on the top of their body near their eyes. These help them breathe when their body is under sand.

Supper with Stingrays

FACT 9

Stingrays don't eat vegetables.

Stingrays are carnivores, which means they only eat meat. The prey a stingray eats depends on where it lives. Some of their favorite meals include shrimp, crabs, clams, oysters, and mussels. Sea worms are also on their menu.

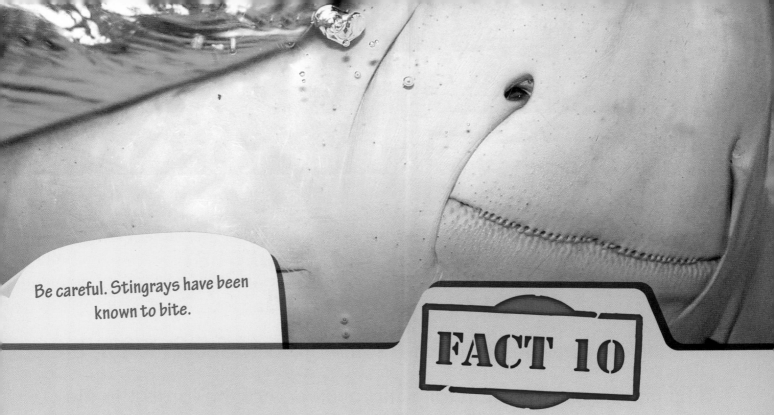

Be careful. Stingrays have been known to bite.

Stingrays have strong jaws for crushing their prey.

With a mouth on its underside, the stingray can easily gobble bottom-dwelling animals, such as crabs and clams. Stingrays have strong jaws to crush their prey. They also have multiple rows of flat teeth for chomping down on hard shells.

Big Fish Story

FACT 11

The short-tail stingray is the largest saltwater stingray in the world.

Stingrays come in all sizes. Some are only about the size of a human hand. The short-tail stingray is one of the largest in the world. It can be over 14 feet (4.3 m) long. Some weigh more than 770 pounds (350 kg).

The giant freshwater stingray is the biggest freshwater fish in the world.

Scientists think the giant freshwater stingray is probably the biggest stingray in the world. It's also believed to be the biggest freshwater fish. It can grow up to 16.5 feet (5 m) long and weigh as much as 1,320 pounds (600 kg).

The round ribbontail ray, shown here, is also known as the giant reef ray.

The 20 Longest Stingrays

name	where it lives	largest size
giant freshwater stingray	rivers in Asia and Oceania	16.5 feet (5 m)
short-tail stingray	Indo-Pacific	14 feet (4.3 m)
leopard whipray	Indo-Pacific	13.5 feet (4.1 m)
thorntail stingray	Indo-Pacific	13.1 feet (4 m)
round ribbontail ray	Indo-Pacific	10.8 feet (3.3 m)
smalleye stingray	Indo-Pacific	10.5 feet (3.2 m)
smalltooth stingray	eastern Atlantic	10.5 feet (3.2 m)
longtail stingray	eastern Pacific	8.5 feet (2.6 m)
round stingray	eastern Atlantic	8.2 feet (2.5 m)
roughtail stingray	eastern Atlantic	7.2 feet (2.2 m)

name	where it lives	largest size
chupare stingray	western central Atlantic	6.6 feet (2 m)
cow stingray	northwest Pacific	6.6 feet (2 m)
longnose stingray	western Atlantic	6.6 feet (2 m)
honeycomb stingray	Indo-Pacific	6.6 feet (2 m)
sharpnose stingray	Indo-Pacific	6.6 feet (2 m)
southern stingray	western Atlantic	6.6 feet (2 m)
whip stingray	western Pacific	6.6 feet (2 m)
whiptail stingray	eastern Pacific	6.1 feet (1.86 m)
cowtail stingray	Indo-Pacific	6 feet (1.83 m)
pink whipray	Indo-Pacific	6 feet (1.83 m)

Sharp Spine!

FACT 13

The stingray can use its tail like a whip.

Stingrays have a long, thin tail with a spine on it. Sometimes stingrays use their tail to swim. Its main use is **defense**. They use their tail as a whip to fight off enemies.

The stingray's spine can be up to 14 inches (36 cm) long.

The barbs sometimes cause a stingray's spine to break off in an enemy. The stingray will then grow a new spine.

FACT 14

The barbed edges of a stingray's spine can be scarier than the spine itself.

Stingray spines are armed with small points called barbs. The barbs point backwards and make the spines hard to remove from flesh. When the stingray pulls its spine out of an enemy, the barbs tear the skin, causing harm and pain. Ow!

A stingray can kill if its spine stabs a major organ, such as the heart.

FACT 15

The stingray can only strike in one direction with its tail.

Stingrays can control how their tail moves. However, when they're ready to strike they need to turn and face their enemy. To attack, the stingray flicks its tail up over its body. The spine whips over the stingray's head and hits the enemy.

FACT 16

Most stingray spines are armed with venom.

Many kinds of stingrays have spines with one or two barbs filled with **venom**. When a stingray strikes an enemy with its spine, the venom enters the enemy's body. The venom is very painful but usually not deadly.

Most people who are attacked by a stingray get spiked in the ankle or lower leg. This happens when someone steps on a hidden stingray while walking through shallow water.

Dentists in ancient Greece used stingray venom to ease pain.

Stingray spines can be useful to humans. People have used stingray spines to make weapons, such as daggers (a kind of knife) and spears. Ancient Greek dentists used the venom on their patients so they would not feel as much pain.

This is a bluespotted stingray.

Sometimes stingrays get their "nails" trimmed.

At some zoos and **aquariums**, you can actually pet a stingray! That may seem like a bad idea. However, before zookeepers let you touch a stingray, they trim the fish's spine, kind of like the way you trim your fingernails. This makes them safe to touch.

Family Time

Female stingrays may not have babies right after mating, but may have them years later.

Mama stingrays usually have babies once a year. A mother usually has a litter of 5 to 15 babies, or pups. The babies grow inside the mother and are pretty big when they're born. Newborn pups look like small adults and can hunt right away.

stingray pup

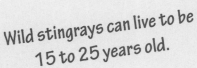
Wild stingrays can live to be 15 to 25 years old.

stingray fossil

Stingrays have been around since the time of the dinosaurs.

For a fish that's been swimming around on this planet for about 95 million years, the stingray hasn't changed much at all. However, the actions of people have harmed the waters where they swim. This means there aren't as many stingrays as there once were.

Strange but Super

Even if you think they look a little weird for fish, stingrays are pretty interesting animals. The venom from their sharp spines can hurt or kill. That same stuff once helped Greeks feel less pain when they went to the dentist!

Scientists are always learning something new about stingrays. The giant freshwater stingray, also called the whipray, was only discovered 20 years ago. Stingrays have been swimming around for millions of years. Hopefully, they'll be around for a lot longer.

The southern stingray, shown here, lives mainly near Florida and the Bahamas.

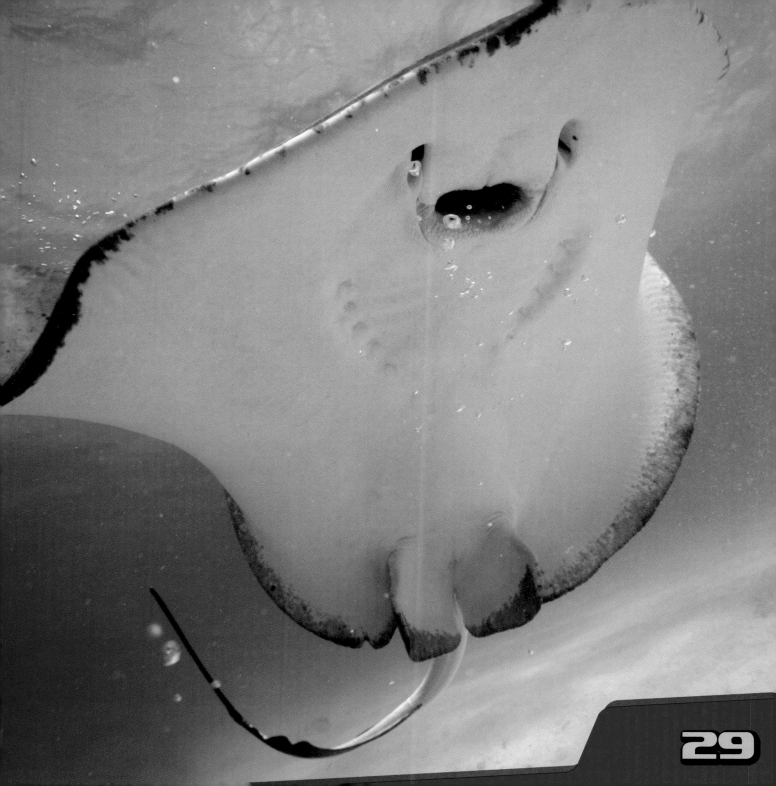

Glossary

aquarium: a zoo for sea animals

defense: the act of resisting an attack

gill: the body part that ocean animals such as fish use to breathe in water

pectoral: on the chest

predator: an animal that hunts other animals for food

prey: an animal that is hunted by other animals for food

sensor: a body part that senses things surrounding the animal

spine: a long, pointy part on an animal

temperate: not too hot or too cold

tropical: having to do with warm areas near the equator

venom: poisonous matter created by an animal and passed on by a bite or sting

For More Information

Books

Coldiron, Deborah. *Stingrays*. Edina, MN: ABDO, 2008.

McFee, Shane. *Stingrays*. New York, NY: PowerKids Press, 2008.

Rustard, Martha E. H. *Stingrays*. Minneapolis, MN: Bellwether Media, 2008.

Websites

How do stingrays kill?
animals.howstuffworks.com/fish/stingray.htm
Learn how stingrays use their tails to defend themselves.

Stingrays
kids.nationalgeographic.com/kids/animals/creaturefeature/stingray/
Learn more about stingrays with fun facts and great photographs.

Index